BABY SEA TURTLE

Published in Canada by Fitzhenry & Whiteside,
195 Allstate Parkway, Markham, Ontario L3R 4T8

Published in the United States by Fitzhenry & Whiteside,
311 Washington Street, Brighton, Massachusetts 02135

www.fitzhenry.ca   godwit@fitzhenry.ca

10 9 8 7 6 5 4 3 2

Library and Archives Canada Cataloguing in Publication

Lang, Aubrey
Baby sea turtle / text by Aubrey Lang ; photography by Wayne Lynch.

(Nature babies)
ISBN-13: 978-1-55041-728-9 (bound)   ISBN-10: 1-55041-728-2 (bound)
ISBN-13: 978-1-55041-746-3 (pbk.)   ISBN-10: 1-55041-746-0 (pbk.)

1. Sea turtles—Infancy—Juvenile literature. I. Lynch, Wayne II. Title. III. Series: Lang, Aubrey. Nature babies.

QL666.C536L35 2007   j597.92'8139   C2006-903249-1

**U.S. Publisher Cataloging-in-Publication Data
(Library of Congress Standards)**

Lang, Aubrey.
Baby sea turtle / Aubrey Lang ; photography by Wayne Lynch.
[36] p. : col. photos. ; cm.   (Nature babies)
Includes index.
Summary: On a narrow strip of beach in Trinidad, a mother sea turtle digs her nest, deposits her eggs and a new life-story begins.
ISBN-10: 1-55041-728-2   ISBN-13: 978-1-55041-728-9
ISBN-1-55041-746-0 (pbk.)   ISBN-13: 978-1-55041-746-3 (pbk.)
1. Sea turtles — Juvenile literature. (1. Sea turtles.) I. Lynch, Wayne. II. Title. III. Series.
597/.92 [E] 22   QL666.C536.L36 2005

Fitzhenry & Whiteside acknowledges with thanks the Canada Council for the Arts, and the Ontario Arts Council
for their support of our publishing program. We acknowledge the financial support of the Government of Canada
through the Book Publishing Industry Development Program (BPIDP) for our publishing activities.

Design by Wycliffe Smith Design Inc.
Printed in Hong Kong

Baby Sea Turtle

WITHDRAWN

Text by Aubrey Lang

Photography by Wayne Lynch

Fitzhenry & Whiteside

BEFORE YOU BEGIN

Hello Young Reader:

To write this book about leatherback sea turtles, we went to the Caribbean island of Trinidad. It was exciting to sit on the beach at night and watch a mother turtle lay her eggs. One turtle got stuck in a big hole on the beach, and she was trapped there until the next day when the hot sun came out. We worried that she might die from the heat. To cool her off, we poured water over her back. Then, with the help of local fishermen, we dragged her out of the hole, and she crawled back to the ocean safely.

We dedicate this book to the scientists and volunteers who work to save endangered sea turtles worldwide. We also wish to thank the Trinidad Wildlife Department and in particular, its director, Mrs. Nadra Nathai-Gyan.

—Aubrey Lang and Wayne Lynch

TABLE OF CONTENTS

The female leatherback sea turtle has traveled a long way to reach the sandy beach where she was born. She swam from the cold waters off the coast of Canada to the warm waters of the Caribbean Sea. The beach is on the island of Trinidad. This is where she will lay her eggs.

She waits until it is dark to come ashore. A large, crashing wave carries her heavy body high up onto the beach. A bright moon rises as she crawls out of the foamy surf.

The female leatherback sea turtle is the largest turtle in the world. She is as big as a single bed, and she weighs more than a refrigerator. Because she is so heavy, she crawls slowly on land and often stops to rest. She doesn't have a hard, scaly shell on her back like other turtles. Instead, she has thick, rubbery skin.

When the mother reaches the top of the beach, she starts to dig. With her long front flippers, she sweeps the sand away from her body and makes a bed for herself. Then, with her back flippers, she starts to scoop out a hole for her eggs. But there is a problem—a log is buried in the sand where she is digging, and she cannot dig deep enough to lay her eggs. She leaves and goes back to the sea.

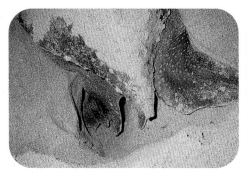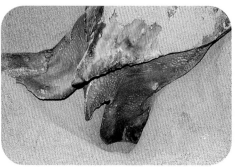

Later in the night, the mother turtle swims to a different part of the beach. This time she finds a perfect place for her nest. She digs a hole that is three feet (0.91 meters) deep, and she lays many eggs. Each egg is about the size of a ping-pong ball. The eggshells are soft, so they don't break when they fall into the hole.

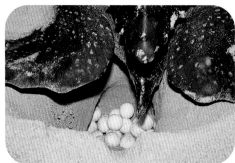

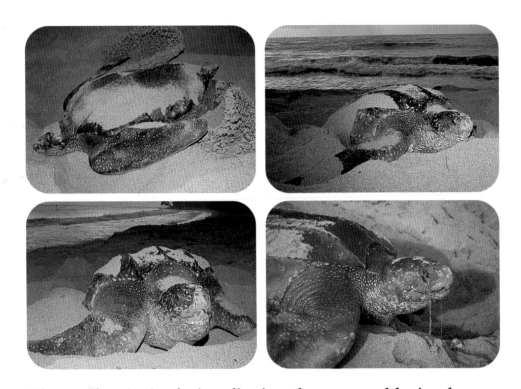

The mother is tired after digging the nest and laying her eggs. But she is not done yet. She must hide the eggs from hungry animals that would eat them, so she spends a long time covering the nest and smoothing out the sand. The thick tears that hang from her eyes make the mother look as if she is crying. But the sticky tears keep her eyes from drying out when she is not in the water.

The same night, many other sea turtles crawl onto the beach to lay their eggs. As the sun comes up, the mother is the last one to leave. Like a bulldozer, she makes deep tracks in the wet sand. She rests in the surf for a few minutes, and then she slowly swims away. She will never see her eggs again.

For two months, the baby turtles have been growing inside the eggs deep beneath the warm sand.

On the night when the eggs begin to hatch, a different mother turtle comes ashore to make a nest for herself. She accidentally digs up the hatching baby turtles and scatters the eggs on top of the sand. Most of them will not survive.

Luckily, a few of the baby turtles hatched before the family nest was disturbed. The hatchlings broke out of the eggs by themselves. Each baby cut a hole in the soft eggshell with a sharp tooth on the end of its nose. Then the young hatchling used its strong front flippers to wiggle out.

Three of the hatchlings circle around, trying to figure out which way to go. On one side of the beach are the dark trees of the jungle; on the other side is the ocean, with the moon shining above it. The baby turtles are so tiny that they can't see the water from where they lie on the sand, but somehow they know they must run toward the bright light of the moon.

Wild dogs and hungry black vultures with sharp beaks hunt on the turtle beach every day. They are looking for eggs that have been disturbed during the night. The vultures and wild dogs will also eat hatchlings, and the babies running toward the ocean are in great danger. The three young turtles reach the water safely, but their little sister is left behind.

The baby sister is stuck in her egg. She struggles to squeeze her way out. She must hurry before the vultures see her. She rests often to build up her strength. One of her flippers is still trapped inside the eggshell, but with a final shove, she pushes her way free and escapes.

In her hurry to get away, the little female heads in the wrong direction and runs into a large log buried in the sand. She tries to climb over the log but falls onto her back. She twists from side to side as she struggles to flip herself over. Finally, she uses her long flippers to turn herself right side up.

The little female finally finds a way around the end of the log, and she heads toward the water. The vultures have not seen her yet, but she faces another problem. A hungry ghost crab lives near the water. Ghost crabs run very fast, and they use their claws to catch baby turtles and drag them into their holes.

Despite all of the dangers on the beach, the little female leatherback finally reaches the surf. A big wave catches her and pulls her into deeper water. For the next day and night, she will swim without stopping—to get as far away from the beach as possible.

Her brothers will never crawl onto the land again. But one night, when the baby leatherback has grown up, she will return to this same beach to lay her eggs.

DID YOU KNOW?

- Worldwide, there are roughly 300 species of turtles and tortoises. Eight of these species are called sea turtles, which live their entire lives in the ocean. Their front legs are shaped like paddles for swimming.

- The leatherback sea turtle is the largest turtle in the world. Adults can grow almost as long as 10 feet (3 meters) and weigh from 550 to 2,000 pounds (250 to 900 kilograms).

- Leatherback sea turtles are among the deepest diving air-breathing animals on the planet. They dive to such depths to search for large jellyfish, a favorite meal. One female dived 3,280 feet (1,000 meters) and held her breath for over an hour.

- The temperature of the surrounding sand determines whether the babies are male or female. When the sand temperature is below 84° Fahrenheit (29° Celsius), eggs develop into male turtles. When the sand is warmer than 86° Fahrenheit (30° Celsius), the eggs hatch out as females. Because temperatures vary within a nest, it usually contains both male and female babies.

- Although leatherback sea turtles nest in the tropics, many of them spend most of their lives in the cold waters of the North Atlantic and northern Pacific. Their large bodies help them to stay warm. An adult leatherback may migrate 9,320 miles (15,000 kilometers) in a single year.

- A mother sea turtle will nest every two or three years and will lay seventy to ninety eggs in each nest. And in a single nesting season, she may return to a beach five or six times to lay eggs.

- Leatherback sea turtles are endangered. Their greatest threats come from fishing nets, in which the sea turtles drown, and egg poaching by humans on the nesting beaches.

INDEX

BIOGRAPHIES

Aubrey Lang and Dr. Wayne Lynch are a husband and wife writer/photographer team. Aubrey has spent the past seventeen years as a freelance writer and photographer. Wayne has been a fulltime science writer and wildlife photographer for twenty-seven years. His images have been published in more than forty countries.

Canadian Wildlife.

Together they've produced over forty titles for children and adults, as well as scripts for television documentaries and countless articles in well-known nature magazines, including *Ranger Rick, Owl, Wild, National Wildlife, Wildlife Conservation, Canadian Geographic,* and